Sir Walter Raleigh

Contents

Signature of
Sir Walter Raleigh.

Introduction

Walter Raleigh's life spans the final years of Mary I's reign, the whole of the Elizabethan era and much of James I's rule. Raleigh witnessed many of the key events of the day. The Tudor period of English History is unquestionably a Golden Age, and this is the story of one of its best-loved characters. This is the tale of one man's ascent from relatively humble origins to international legend. To many, Walter Raleigh was a pirate, traitor, scholar, coloniser, explorer, soldier, poet, adventurer, scientist, cartographer, botanist, fashionista and Favourite of a queen. He is credited with introducing tobacco and potatoes to England. Although not everything he did resulted in success, his exploits never lacked ambition or self-confidence. He left his mark on England, parts of Europe and America.

A 19th-century tablet marking his grave in St Margaret's Church, Westminster states:

> *'Reader should you reflect on his errors,*
> *Remember his many virtues*
> *and that he was mortal.'*

This is his story.

Did you know?

Raleigh is pronounced – "RAW LEE" rather than Raleigh, as in the bicycle manufacturer.

Contemporaries sometimes spelt it Ralegh.

'I have heard but rawly of thee' said James I, making a pun of his name.

There are 73 different contemporary spellings of his name but for this book we shall use RALEIGH.

Statue outside Sherborne Abbey.

The Early Years

A West Country Man

Walter Raleigh was born at Hayes Barton, East Budleigh in Devon around 1552–54 into an established county family. He was the second son of Katherine Champernowne and Walter Raleigh senior, a gentleman farmer. Both his parents had been married before and he was brought up in a large extended family. Walter's early years were spent in Devon where he was tutored by the local vicar. It is said that he spoke with a broad Devonshire accent to his dying day. He was brought up in the Protestant faith and spent an idyllic childhood playing in the beautiful Devon countryside by the sea.

Mentors and Circle of Influence

Raleigh's circle of influence included his half-brothers: Adrian Gilbert, the notable surveyor, seaman and courtier, and Sir Humphrey Gilbert, explorer and holder of a royal patent to discover new lands. His cousins included Henry Champernowne, soldier and champion of the Huguenot cause, Sir Richard Grenville, explorer, soldier and privateer, and Sir Francis Drake, sailor and the first Englishman to circumnavigate the globe. His aunt, Katherine Astley, was the governess to Elizabeth I from 1547.

His father, also Walter, was an established country gentleman and a Protestant, holding the offices of acting Vice-Admiral in Devon and member of parliament for Wareham in Dorset. These people and their interests helped to shape young Walter's fate and passions in later life.

Above: A Signpost in East Budleigh of Hayes Barton, birthplace of Sir Walter.

Left: Sir Humphrey Gilbert.

Oxford and Soldiering in France

Oriel College, Oxford

As a younger son, Raleigh was expected to make his own way in the world. In 1568, at the age of 16, he followed in the footsteps of many of his class and continued his education at Oriel College, Oxford. Here he proved himself as an academic and wit. Like so many students to come, he had problems with student debt.

John Aubrey records a story told by Thomas Child of Worcestershire that he 'borrowed a Gowne of him when he was at Oxford … which he never restored, nor money for it'.

It is uncertain if Raleigh graduated from Oxford, but there is no doubt that it was here he gained a life-long love of learning.

Soldiering in France

In France, the Catholics were fighting the Protestant Huguenots. Raleigh – egged on by his kinsman Henry Champernowne, an experienced soldier – dropped out of university and joined him on the Huguenot side. He proved to be a useful soldier and fought in 1569 in both the Battle of Jarnac and the Battle of Moncontour. Here he learnt valuable combat and man-management skills. He spent between two and three years fighting on the continent before finally returning to England.

Oriel College, Oxford where Raleigh studied. Undergraduates in Tudor times could be as young as 10 or as old as 25.

Middle Temple, London.

Middle Temple

In 1575, Raleigh returned to England to read Law at Middle Temple. It would seem that he never intended to practise Law, but this was a well-trodden route for the life of a courtier. Instead, this was more of a cultural journey, for Raleigh learnt to sing and dance, as well as how to behave in polite society. It was here that his poetry was first to draw acclaim, for it came to the attention of George Gascoigne who included some of Raleigh's pieces in his book, *The Steele Glass*, published in 1576.

Sir Edward Coke was to taunt him at his trial for lack of legal experience. Raleigh replied:

'If I ever read a word of the law or statutes before I was a prisoner in the Tower, God confound me!'

First Seafaring Voyage to Discover the Northwest Passage

At the age of 26, in 1578, he joined his half-brother Humphrey Gilbert on an abortive voyage of discovery across the Atlantic to find the Northwest Passage, captaining the Queen's 100-ton ship, the *Falcon*. The plan was to sail to the coast of North America and to see if there was a route around the top of the continent through the Arctic Ocean before heading south to India and China. It was probably this voyage that first brought Raleigh's name to the attention of Elizabeth I.

The expedition was thwarted from the start. On leaving the Azores, Humphrey Gilbert's fleet of seven ships was blown back to port by strong winds. The damaged and repaired ships set out again into winter storms. One ship deserted and returned to England. The Spanish (who were also in the area) were convinced that the expedition would attack their ships and possessions; relations between Spain and

The *Falcon*, captained by Raleigh, carrying 7 gentlemen, and 60 mariners and soldiers. Their motto was 'I neither seek death, nor flee mine end'.

England were strained during this period. A fierce battle took place off Cape Verde, during which Raleigh was nearly killed and many men were lost. Raleigh returned to Falmouth in May 1579.

It was on this voyage that Raleigh first established his reputation as an explorer and adventurer.

Acts of Piracy

Soon after they returned home, Raleigh and Humphrey Gilbert were investigated by the Privy Council for acts of piracy nearer to home. A Spanish ship laden with oranges and lemons had been captured and taken to Torbay where the goods were sold, and it was believed that Raleigh and Gilbert were involved. There wasn't enough evidence, though, and the charges were dropped. Throughout Raleigh's life there are many accusations and complaints concerning his sea captains and deputies from ship owners in France, Spain, Portugal and the Netherlands. Correspondence from the ambassadors of Spain, France, Venice and the King of Spain cite him as the greatest menace after Francis Drake.

Piracy was common in Elizabethan times.

Ireland

The Desmond Rebellions

From 1579–83, Raleigh was involved in the bloody crushing of the Desmond Rebellions. These were uprisings against Elizabeth's suppression of the feudal system in Ireland as well as the requisition of Irish lands for English settlers. The traditional feudal lords of Ireland resisted not only the reduction of their influence but also the threat to Catholicism in Ireland. In Cork, Raleigh tried Sir James Fitzgerald, the younger brother of the Earl of Desmond and one of the leaders of the rebellion, on a charge of treason. Fitzgerald was found guilty and was hung, drawn and quartered. It was Raleigh's men who cut up his body into tiny pieces. At the Siege of Smerwick in County Kerry, his troops were responsible for the slaughter of about 600 Italian and Spanish soldiers who were fighting for the Catholic cause.

Raleigh's Irish Acquisitions

Upon the successful quashing of the Rebellion, Raleigh was rewarded with 40,000 acres in Munster, including the coastal walled towns of Lismore and Youghal. At Killua Castle, Clonmellon in County Westmeath, he was to plant the first potatoes that he imported to Ireland. He was mayor here from 1588–89. He chose Myrtle Grove in Youghal as his town house, although he based himself at Lismore Castle. He was also given Barryscourt and the Great Island – lands previously belonging to the Barry family.

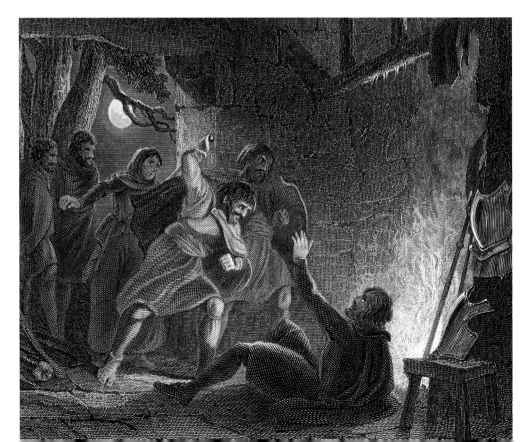

Lismore Castle, County Waterford.

As well as potatoes, he also introduced a strong smelling yellow wall flower from the Azores and the "Affane Cherry", which he gathered from his expeditions to the Canary Islands.

Despite being one of the largest land holders in Ireland, he had very little success in persuading English settlers to come as tenants for his land. In 1602, when his estates ran into financial difficulties, Raleigh was forced to sell his Irish lands to Richard Boyle, 1st Earl of Cork.

Left: The Desmond Rebellion.

Alice Goold

Whilst in Ireland, Raleigh had a daughter with a local woman, Alice Goold. Although, they never married, she was mentioned in his will. She in fact predeceased him, dying of plague in Kingston, Surrey. His daughter went on to marry his ward and page from Jersey, Daniel Dumaresq, Seigneur de Saumarez. Raleigh was an astute enough man to know that if he married, he needed to marry a lady of substance, breeding and connections to advance his career.

Life at Court and Capturing Elizabeth I's Eye

Raleigh lays his cloak across a puddle for Elizabeth I.

Greenwich Palace

Elizabeth's Court was based in Greenwich in 1580 and Raleigh was amongst the young men who flocked to it. Here he established a reputation as a bit of a lad. He was called three times before the Privy Council for brawling. One incident involved a brawl with Edward Wingfield on a tennis court in Westminster. He was briefly jailed for his behaviour.

The Famous Cloak Legend

In 1580, Elizabeth was 47 years old and unmarried. She loved the company of bright and handsome young men. Legend has it that one day, as she approached a puddle, Raleigh rushed forward with his cloak and laid it on the ground so she could continue with dry feet. This act of gallantry caught the Queen's eye, and she took Raleigh under her wing. He soon established himself as a firm friend and close confidant. Elizabeth promoted him to Esquire of the Body Extraordinary.

Robert Naunton, a contemporary, noted: 'He had gotten the Queen's ear in a trice' and that Elizabeth held Raleigh, 'for a kinde of oracle, which nettled them all'.

You can see from this portrait that he is wearing fine furs, a doublet of silk and a pearl earring.

Aubrey: 'a most remarkable aspect, an exceedingly high forehead, long faced, and sour eie-lidded a kind a pigge-eie' and his beard 'turned up naturally.'

Naunton: 'In the outward man, a good presence, in a bold plausible tongue, whereby he could set out his parts to the best advantage.'

This was an entry level role for an aspiring courtier and involved the duties of dogsbody and general errand runner. Timing was opportune. Elizabeth's Favourite, Robert Dudley, Earl of Leicester had fallen from grace upon his marriage to the widowed Countess of Essex. The fall of Leicester produced a vacancy, and Raleigh was quick to fill the shoes of the Favourite.

Elizabeth's Eye Candy

In 1580, Raleigh was 28 years old and exceedingly handsome. He was six feet tall, swarthy, dark-haired, bearded, dashing, witty and confident. John Aubrey remarked that the Queen liked to have 'proper men' about her. Raleigh had all the attributes to fit this requirement, and he certainly stepped up to the mark.

Above: Elizabethan parrying dagger.

The Fashionista

Raleigh was aware of the importance of good appearance and all the contemporary portraits of him show a fashionably dressed man. It was said that he spent up to an hour a day combing his hair. In Elizabethan England, clothes not only functioned to keep you warm, they also conveyed your wealth, education and status. In her will, Elizabeth bequeathed the sleeves of her dresses to her ladies-in-waiting – whence came the expression of 'wearing one's wealth on one's sleeve'.

Tudor clothes were cleverly designed and each garment was in several parts. In an age before zips and fasteners, people were often sewn into their clothes. Sleeves could be worn with different outfits; thus a mix and match approach was used.

A glove owned by Walter Raleigh.

Raleigh's tobacco pouch.

Favourite, Friend ... and Lover?

Raleigh was quick to win the Queen's trust and favour. She nicknamed him 'Water', a play on his name and his maritime interests. Elizabeth enjoyed his quick wit and sense of humour. They soon formed an easy rapport and strong bond. This can be seen in poetry they sent each other.

The age-old question of whether they were lovers may never be resolved. However, it is fair to say that Elizabeth highly prized Raleigh's company and valued his presence at all times. She forbade him to go to America to head his own expedition in 1595, and her furious reaction to his secret marriage to Bess Throckmorton, one of her ladies-in-waiting in 1591, does seem to reveal the sentiments of a jealous lover.

Rise of Status, Wealth and Power

In 1583, when Raleigh was about 31, Elizabeth granted him a lease of Durham House on the Strand overlooking the River Thames. Raleigh lived there until the Queen's death in 1603, and spent the enormous sum of £2,000 on renovations. Raleigh's study was in a turret that overlooked the Thames and had a view of Westminster, Whitehall Palace and the Surrey hills. From here, he could also view his ships.

Durham House presented in the bottom left of the image.

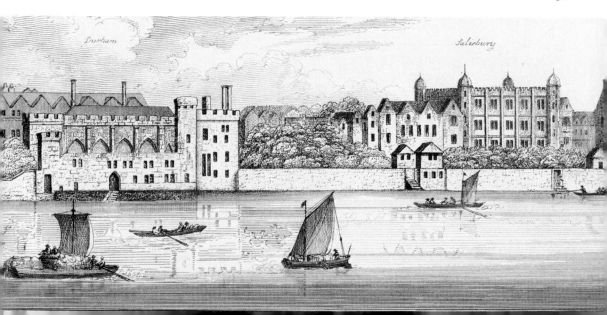

> *'Fain would I climb,*
> *yet fear I to fall'*

Sir Walter Raleigh

> *'If thy heart fails thee,*
> *climb not at all'*

Elizabeth I

Poetry written by Walter Raleigh and Elizabeth I. This was etched into a diamond shaped window pane. Sir Walter Raleigh wrote the first line with a diamond ring and Elizabeth wrote the following.

Patronages, Monopolies and Gifts

In recognition of his growing esteem in the eyes of Elizabeth, Raleigh was granted various patronages and monopolies that led to great wealth. In 1583, he was given the manors of Stolney and Newland, and in May of that year, she granted him the 'Farm of Wines', which meant that every vintner had to pay Raleigh an annual retail licence of £1. In 1584, he was granted the right to export undyed cloth. All exporting merchants were obliged to pay Raleigh a tax on every yard of cloth sold. As Warden of the Stanneries, he had the lucrative task of controlling the tin mines in Devon and Cornwall. He was also granted patents on the manufacture of playing cards.

Upon the failure of the Babington Plot in 1586, which aimed to assassinate Elizabeth and enthrone Mary, Queen of Scots, all of Anthony Babington's assets were confiscated by the Crown, and Raleigh was given an impressive list of properties and land in Lincolnshire, Derbyshire and Nottinghamshire – including a house called Babbington Hall in Lincolnshire. Raleigh also became one of the most powerful men in the west, becoming Vice-Admiral of Devon and Cornwall, Lord Lieutenant of Cornwall and an MP.

Playing Card, Queen of Hearts.

Royal Appointments

In 1585 Raleigh was knighted, and in the summer of 1587, he was appointed Captain of the Yeomen of the Guard, which made him responsible for the Queen's safety. He was to be at her side constantly and this marked the apex of his career. As he was a bit of a maverick and wild card, the role of a Privy Councillor was, however, denied him.

America

Patent to Explore the New World

In 1584, Raleigh was granted by Elizabeth a patent to explore the New World. Spain and Portugal both had colonies in the New World, but England's colonial activities had been restricted to Ireland.

Several reasons can be cited for Raleigh's desire to explore. It offered him the chance to discover gold and treasure and to acquire great personal wealth; to make a lasting impression on Queen Elizabeth I and increase her dominions; to establish a base for raids on the Spanish, and to find adventure while satisfying his own personal curiosity about the wider world.

First Reconnaissance Mission

In 1584, Philip Amadas and Arthur Barlow commanded the *Bark Ralegh* and the *Dorothy*, respectively. Raleigh oversaw the equipping of the ships and sponsored the manufacture and design of the navigational instruments, but did not sail with them. The ships set sail on 27th April 1584. They landed on the island of Hatarask, off what is now North Carolina. Here, they met local Native Americans, with whom they got on well, and exchanged goods. Six weeks later, they returned to the West Country carrying promising tales, two members of the Algonquin tribe called Manteo and Wanchese, and a rich and varied cargo.

Manteo and Wanchese stayed at Durham House and quickly made a sensation at Court. Raleigh's priority, however, was not publicity but rather intelligence about his new land of Virginia – named by Raleigh in honour of his patron, Elizabeth, the Virgin Queen. The scientist, Thomas Hariot, was tasked with deciphering and learning the Algonquian language. The Native Americans raised the profile of Raleigh's plans and funding for further trips was made available.

Raleigh:
'There are stranger things to be seen in the world than are between London and Stanes.'

Watercolour painting by Governor John White
c.1585 of a Native American.

Fleet of the Second Expedition
Ships, Commanders and Key Passengers

Tyger, 160-ton ship: commanded by Sir Richard Grenville – Admiral and General;
Simon Fernandez – Master and Chief Pilot of the Fleet;
Ralph Lane – Governor Designate of Virginia; Francis Brooke – Treasurer;
Philip Amadas – Vice-Admiral and Admiral of Virginia Designate

Raleigh's own *Roebuck* – commanded by John Clarke
Dorothy – commanded by Arthur Barlow
Red Lion – commanded by George Raymond
Elizabeth – commanded by Thomas Cavendish, the expedition's High Marshall

Two pinnaces were carried aboard as tenders

Second Expedition to Establish a Colony – 9th April 1585

Elizabeth forbade Raleigh from accompanying this voyage for she did not want to risk her Favourite on such a hazardous journey. Raleigh was therefore to be the mastermind, main financier and fixer. The expedition consisted of 600 men, of whom 300 were mariners, and the rest were a range of highly skilled craftsmen: apothecaries, brick-makers, carpenters, factors and farmers. Thomas Hariot accompanied the voyage to be in charge of relations with the Native Americans. John White was assigned the role of cartographer.

The Journey

Storms resulted in the loss of both pinnaces off Portugal and the fleet scattered, regrouping in Puerto Rico. They sailed via Hispaniola and the Bahamas, and up the Florida Channel. Here, the *Tyger* grounded, losing valuable provisions. Grenville decided to put ashore, and they discovered sunflowers and pumpkins growing there as well as tobacco, which the natives were observed to smoke.

Armed with these facts, the expedition decided to build a settlement on Roanoke Island. About 107 men were left there to establish a colony, and Grenville returned on the *Tyger* to England. On the way home, he captured the Spanish ship, the *Santa Maria* – containing gold, silver, spices, pearls, sugar and its crew – and brought it back to England as a prize for ransom. Both Elizabeth and Raleigh were delighted with these spoils and the encouraging news of the new settlement.

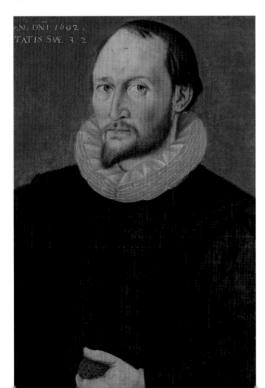

Thomas Hariot, ethnographer and scientist.

The lost colony of Roanoke.

Roanoke Island

A fort was built on the island, containing a store, guardroom and magazine. The settlers were entirely reliant on the native Americans for provisions and food as those brought from England lasted only twenty days. Corn could only be planted in the following spring. Relations with the local tribes soon deteriorated and the settlers longed to go home.

Raleigh planned to send a relief ship in November 1585, but this was delayed and did not sail until after Easter 1586.

Sir Francis Drake.

Sir Francis Drake

In the meantime, Drake visited Roanoke in the *Francis* after his successful piracy acts against the Spanish off the Florida Coast. The settlers were desperate to return home and, in their haste to join Drake's ship, many maps, books, papers and botanical specimens were lost. They returned to Portsmouth on 27th July 1586. The relief ship finally arrived shortly after Drake's departure and found the settlement abandoned. Fifteen men were left to keep a foothold in the new colony and the ship returned to England.

The Lost Colony

In 1587, Raleigh despatched John White, whom he appointed Governor, and a further 115 colonists to establish a colony on Chesapeake Bay. The party arrived at Roanoke on 22nd July 1587, to find no signs of life – just a skeleton. White attempted to re-establish relations with the Native Americans, which had been soured the previous year. Unfortunately, these attempts were abortive. Some of the frightened colonists begged to return to England. White set sail in late 1587 leaving behind 90 men, 17 women and 11 children and his granddaughter Virginia Dare – the first English child to be born in America.

Plans for a relief mission were delayed by the winter and the deterioration of relations with Spain. The ensuing Armada resulted in the sequestration of all ships by the Crown. White finally returned to Roanoke on his granddaughter's third birthday, 18th August 1590, where he found a deserted settlement that had been dismantled – not abandoned – in a hurry. The only clue was 'Croatoan' written on a fence post. He took this to mean that the settlers had moved to Croatoan Island, but he was unable to commence a search as the weather changed.

Raleigh's Final Expedition

Twelve years later, in 1602, Raleigh sent a final expedition, led by Samuel Mace, to discover what had happened to his colony. He hoped to make money from the trip by collecting aromatic woods and plants such as sassafras, which were very richly prized at home. The weather turned before they could reach Roanoke and they were forced to return to England.

Lasting Impact on Raleigh's Colonial Expedition

To some, the colony was seen as a failure. But it could be regarded as a success, for it showed that the English could survive in the wilderness for almost a year and the horizons of the English imperial vision had been extended. England had claimed its first foothold in the New World, and today the capital of North Carolina is named Raleigh in his honour. Maize, tobacco and potatoes were introduced into England and their popularity increased. The colony had failed due to a lack of leadership, clashes of personalities, aggressive relations with the Native Americans and poor timing for the planting of crops. Also, many of the early colonists were paid and did not have the personal conviction of later expeditions such as those who travelled out in the *Mayflower*. It could be argued that Raleigh laid the foundations of the British Empire.

Christening of Virginia Dare – the first English person to be born in America.

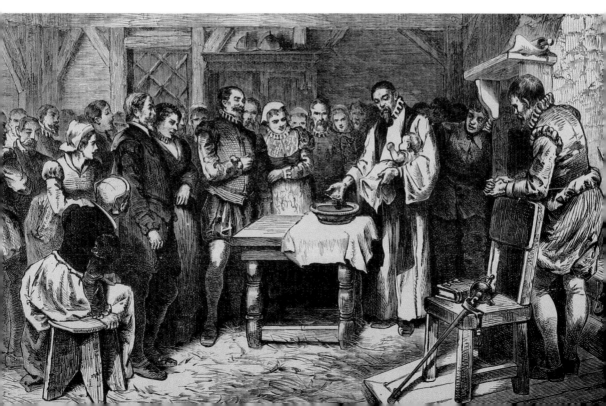

A Country Estate
and a Home

Raleigh's land and property acquisitions grew with time. Although he possessed lands in Ireland and Oxfordshire, and a house in London, what Raleigh really wanted was to have a home becoming of his new-found status. Most of his interests lay in the West Country, and thus he initially sought to acquire Hayes Barton, his old family home. Unsuccessful in this, his eyes turned to another property.

Sherborne Castle (now known as Sherborne Old Castle)

According to an account written by Sir John Harrington, Raleigh first saw Sherborne Castle as he was riding past on the road between Plymouth and London. This 12th-century castle, owned by the Bishop of Salisbury, stood

On the left is Raleigh's original Castle (now called Sherborne Old Castle) and on the right is Sherborne Lodge, the house he modified and built, now called Sherborne Castle.

on a mound above the river Yeo, surrounded by a deer park and ringed by ancient woodland.

He turned in his saddle to point out the view to his companions and this startled his horse, which caused Raleigh to fall to the ground. Laughing, he scrambled to his feet saying that he had taken physical hold of the land he coveted. Raleigh used his influence with Elizabeth to persuade her that he was worthy of such a prize. He presented her with a jewel worth £250 to attain his goal. When the Bishopric of Salisbury next became vacant, she appointed a candidate on the condition that he would grant her a lease of Sherborne Castle and its estates. This lease she transferred to Raleigh in 1592.

Harrington records that Raleigh 'cast such an eye upon it as Ahab did upon Naboth's vineyard'.

Sherborne Lodge in Raleigh's Time.

Grand Modernising Plans

Raleigh immediately set about an ambitious modernising campaign. To the gatehouse, he added two square-headed windows, and inside he installed new chimney pieces. However, the difficulties and expense of modernising a 12th-century building were very great and Raleigh decided to build a new house situated across the valley in the deer park.

Sherborne Lodge (now known as Sherborne Castle)

A hunting lodge had been built in the park *c*.1500 by the Bishops of Salisbury, and this was to be the site of Raleigh's new house. The new house was rectangular, four storeys high, with rendered walls, ogee gables and large square windows filled with diamond-pane glass. It was one of the new Elizabethan lodges, built light and airy like a tower house, designed for gracious living within and to impress from without.

Modernised and Personalised with the Latest Fashions

Raleigh's hand can be seen in many aspects of the Castle. He was very much involved in the design and layout of house and garden. He wanted not only a prestigious house but a comfortable one. Throughout the house, Raleigh personalised the interior with his coat of arms, five lozenges and his device of a buck.

Sir Walter Raleigh:
Sherborne Castle was,
'my fortune's fold'

Raleigh, the Landscape Gardener and Plantsman

When Raleigh acquired Sherborne Lodge, it was surrounded by a deer park. With the help of his half-brother, Adrian Gilbert – the renowned Tudor garden designer – the grounds around the Lodge were transformed. Raleigh planted exotics brought back from his expeditions overseas. They laid out gardens, which included pools, canals and waterfalls. To the east of the Lodge, a Parlour Garden was installed to a formal design.

Raleigh's seat still survives, built against the park wall, so he could watch the traffic on the main road, whilst enjoying the view over his gardens. It was here that he liked to sit and smoke his pipe and where an anxious servant is reputed to have doused him with ale, thinking he was on fire!

Raleigh being doused with ale by a servant.

Raleigh's seat.

Potatoes and Tobacco

Raleigh is best known for introducing these to England from Virginia. He may not have been the *first* to introduce tobacco or potatoes, but he certainly made smoking the latest fashion. He grew potatoes on his estates in Ireland and at Checcombe, Sherborne.

'Sir Walter Rawleighe .... beautified [his Park] with Orchardes, Gardens and Groves of much Varietie and great Delight; soe that, whether you consider the Pleasantnesse of the Seate, the Goodnesse of the Soyle, or the other Delicacies belongeing unto it, it rests unparalleled by anie in these partes.'

Coker's Survey of Dorset, 1620

Trial for Atheism
'The School of Night'

The most notorious event of Raleigh's life in Sherborne was his trial for atheism, which took place at Cerne Abbas in 1594. A charge of atheism was nearly the equivalent of treason, since the monarch was the Head of the Church and to be against the Church was to be against the monarch.

Circle of Free-thinking Friends

Raleigh, a true Renaissance man, had gathered together at Sherborne a circle of free-thinking friends and relatives – including the astronomer John Dee, the seaman Lawrence Keymis, Thomas Hariot, the mathematician, Adrian Gilbert, his half-brother who was a chemist and explorer, and his brother, Carew.

The Trial

Raleigh was accused of conducting a 'School of Atheism' or a 'School of Night' at Sherborne

Lodge and several local witnesses came forward to testify, including Robert Hyde, a shoemaker, who alleged:

'There is a company about this town that sayeth that Hell is no other but poverty and penury in this world, and Heaven is no other than to be rich and enjoy pleasures, and that we die like beasts.'

The Vicar of Sherborne, Francis Scarlett, and one of the churchwardens also spoke at the trial. The trial was dismissed through a lack of evidence but it left a stain on Raleigh's character.

Raleigh's study where he entertained his friends.

Raleigh's Role in the Armada, 1588

The threat of a Spanish invasion loomed darkly over much of Elizabeth's reign. By 1585, English relations with Spain had reached a new low. Philip II of Spain ordered all English ships in Spanish ports to be seized, their cargoes impounded, the crews imprisoned and all cannon to be sent to Cadiz. Raleigh's expedition to the New World was tasked with warning English fishermen off the coast of Newfoundland not to take their catches into Spanish ports. After the execution of Mary, Queen of Scots in February 1587, Philip II of Spain had a direct claim to the English throne – being the widowed husband of Elizabeth's sister, Mary I.

What was the Spanish Armada?

The Spanish Armada was a fleet of 130 ships, which set sail from Spain in 1588 with the purpose of escorting an army from the Spanish Netherlands to invade England. The strategic aim was to overthrow Queen Elizabeth and the Tudor establishment of Protestantism and restore the Catholic Church in England. It was also hoped that this would put a stop to English interference in the Spanish Netherlands and end the harm caused to Spanish interests by English and Dutch privateers.

The Armada.

130 ships left La Coruna in August 1588.

Raleigh and the Council of War

As Lord Lieutenant of Cornwall and Vice-Admiral of Devon and Cornwall, Raleigh was a member of the Council of War. The Council met to consider the defence of the realm. Key places along the coast were to be fortified, and Raleigh was charged with fortifying strategic places in Devon, Dorset and Cornwall, including those at Plymouth, Portland and Weymouth. He helped raise 2,000 foot soldiers and acquire 200 horses.

His Actual Role in the Armada

This remains unclear but he certainly provided his own ship *Ark Ralegh*, which he sold to the Crown in 1587 and this was renamed the *Ark Royal*. His main contributions were to the land defences and the advice he gave to the Council of War. He may have fought a sea battle off Portland on 23rd July 1588, but this cannot be fully substantiated. His ships, the *Roebuck* and *Revenge*, captured the Spanish ship *Rosario* and took her to Dartmouth where the crew helped themselves to the coffers containing gold cloth and furniture. Months later the government authorities were still pursuing these cargoes, and it would seem that Raleigh did not miss the opportunity to profit from this venture.

The Defeat of the Armada

Legend has it that Sir Francis Drake was playing bowls on Plymouth Hoe when word reached him that an Armada of ships was sighted off The Lizard in Cornwall. Drake is reported to have said that there was time enough to finish the game and beat the Spanish too. The English fleet set sail from Plymouth. Fireships were sent in by the English. Helped by a strong wind, a wall of fire was created, causing panic and disarray amongst the Spanish. The English attacked again and the Spanish fleet was split up. The English ships were faster and more agile than the Spanish, and the captains – who were mainly from the West Country – knew the seas well. With stormy seas and the loss of two thousand men in just one week, the Spanish retreated. Just 63 of the original 130 ships limped home to Spain.

The defeat of the Armada was a key moment in Elizabeth's reign. The Protestant faith was safeguarded, the reputation of the English fleet was enhanced and the victory marked the decline in the power of Spain.

Ark Royal, formally the *Ark Ralegh*.

Secret Marriage

The Court was full of eligible young ladies in want of a husband. Raleigh was astute enough to realise that his role as Elizabeth's Favourite required absolute loyalty. He would have witnessed her displeasure when her previous Favourites, Cecil and Essex, had married without her consent. However, in 1591 Raleigh defied Elizabeth and secretly married her lady-in-waiting, Elizabeth Throckmorton. Bess was no heiress or particular beauty, but this was a love match and they remained happily married until Raleigh's death. They were to have three sons, Damerei, Walter (Wat) and Carew.

The Queen first became aware in May 1592 of the secret marriage and of the birth of Damerei. She was furious and placed Bess and Raleigh under house arrest, before sending them to the Tower of London. It was not unusual for the Queen's Favourites to be confined at the Queen's pleasure without trial.

Life in the Tower

Although Raleigh was confined to Brick Tower, life was relatively comfortable. The Raleighs could receive visitors, correspond and carry out business. Raleigh even continued his duties as Captain of the Yeomen of the Guard through his deputies.

Madre de Dios

Attempts to regain favour with Elizabeth initially failed. However, Raleigh was able to ransom himself out of the Tower after two months when one of his ships captured the Spanish ship *Madre de Dios* with a very rich cargo. Raleigh was released from the Tower to take charge of the treasure. His share was meagre but reflected the price he had to pay for marrying Bess. Bess was released in December 1592, joining her husband at Sherborne. Elizabeth expected the couple to sue for pardon, but they refused and Raleigh remained out of favour for five years. Bess was never received back at Court.

Elizabeth (Bess) Raleigh née Throckmorton.

El Dorado

Stories of a legendary City of Gold – an 'El Dorado' – in Guiana, South America, abounded. Raleigh had a long been fascinated by these tales and wished to claim it for England. He hoped that finding such a prize would cause Elizabeth to forgive him and welcome him back to Court. On 6th February 1595, Raleigh set sail with a fleet of six ships. He explored what is now called Venezuela and Guiana. Although, he failed to find the City of Gold, he sailed up the Orinoco River and learnt of silver mines; he brought back samples of ore, which proved to be fool's gold.

The Final Years of Elizabeth's Reign

On 1st July 1597, he was finally welcomed back to Court, but Raleigh's ambitions to be a Privy Councillor were never fulfilled. Elizabeth saw that he lacked the qualities of a council member and, although she sought his advice in private, his hot-headedness prevented him from further advancement to councillor. Nevertheless, he was never truly removed from her favour right up until her death on 24th March 1603, at the then great age of 65.

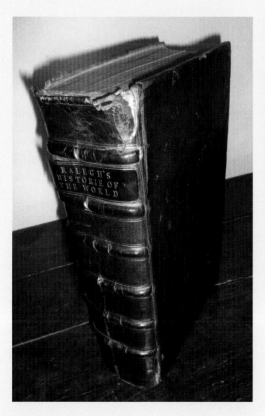

Raleigh the Travel Writer

To counter any expression of doubt that he actually visited South America, he documented his travels in his books *The Discoverie of the Large, Rich, and Bewtiful Empyre of Guiana*, published first in 1596, and *The Discovery of Guiana, and The Journal of the Second Voyage Thereto*, published in 1606.

Both became bestsellers and William Shakespeare is said to have used them for research.

Whilst imprisoned in the Tower of London, Raleigh wrote many treatises, including the first volume of *The Historie of the World*, where he explored the ancient history of Greece and Rome.

A Decline in Fortunes

News of Elizabeth's death was relayed to Edinburgh, and on 5th April, James VI of Scotland took up the English throne as James I. Various courtiers had sought James's favour in the last years of Elizabeth's reign but Raleigh was not one of these. They were polar opposites. James was determined to stamp his own mark on the monarchy and disassociate himself with the previous regime. It soon became apparent to everyone but Raleigh that he could never expect any favours from the King. James soon stripped him of all his monopolies and ordered him to quit Durham House immediately.

Implicated in a plot to place Lady Arbella Stuart – a possible successor to Queen Elizabeth I – on the throne, Raleigh was thrown in the Tower, under sentence of death. Wracked with despair, he attempted to take his own life by stabbing himself in the chest. Public state trials for treason were a foregone conclusion and he was found guilty. He was sentenced to be hung, drawn and quartered.

Writing desk in the Tower.

Bedroom in the Bloody Tower.

The Bloody Tower.

Life in the Tower of London, 1603–16

Fortunately for Raleigh, his sentence was transmuted to life imprisonment and he remained confined to apartments in the Bloody Tower until 1616. His accommodation was reasonably comfortable, although he complained of the damp, which affected his health. He was able to receive visitors and scholars, was able to correspond with the outside world and he continued his studies. A studious atmosphere prevailed. Bess was able to join him, and their son, Carew, was born here in 1605.

The Trust Deed of 1603.

*'for so long tyme
as yt shall please
Almighty God
remayne, contyewe,
be discende in the name
and blood of the said
Sir Walter Ralegh'*

Medicine Man and Chemist

In the Tower, Raleigh wrote many treatises and began writing an ambitious undertaking, *The Historie of the World*. The first volume was published 1614 and a further two volumes were never finished. He was also able to grow herbs in a garden and undertake scientific experiments. When Queen Anne, James I's wife, became ill, Raleigh gave him some of his famous cordial which cured her.

Tutor to Henry, Prince of Wales

Raleigh became friendly with Queen Anne, whom instructed him to tutor her son, Henry. He was more than qualified to do this and able to teach the young prince science, history, politics, shipbuilding and navigation. Henry died unexpectedly of typhoid in 1612 at the age of 18, and this was a great blow to Raleigh.

Henry, Prince of Wales, 1594–1612.

Everything that Raleigh had striven for and achieved was snatched from him whilst in the Tower. His main sources of income were cut off. He was stripped of the Governorship of Jersey, the Wardenship of the Stanneries, the wine patents, Rangerships of the New Forest, the Lieutenancy of Portland Castle and the seal of the Duchy of Cornwall. He received £300 in compensation but lost an income of £3,000.

Sherborne Estates

In 1599, Elizabeth had converted Raleigh's lease into a freehold, giving him full ownership of the estates at Sherborne. In 1603, he made strenuous legal efforts to secure this for future generations by drawing up a Trust Deed in favour of his heirs. Unfortunately, a crucial phrase was found to be missing and, in a cruel twist of fate, Raleigh was forced to surrender the estates to the Crown. James I gave this to his favourite, Robert Carr.

A Cordial Water of Sir Walter Raleigh

Bezoar Stone, hart's horn, ammonia, ground pearl, musk, spirts of wine, with mint, borage, gentian sugar, sassafras and assorted spices.

Decline and Fall

Second Attempt to Find El Dorado, 1617

Raleigh continued to protest his innocence. He regularly petitioned James I and offered him advice on a range of subjects. The Crown's finances were in a dire state, and Raleigh asked James to allow him to undertake another expedition to find El Dorado. James never pardoned Raleigh, but allowed him out of the Tower on licence. Raleigh sunk much of what was left of his fortune into this trip. Many people thought he would disappear or go pirating. Relations with Spain were at a sensitive level, and Raleigh was specifically ordered not to engage with Spanish troops.

Raleigh set sail from London in the *Destiny* and a fleet of ships. He was accompanied by his son Wat and 431 men. The fleet encountered rough seas and many of the crew grew sick; Raleigh was struck down with fever. They landed at Cayenne in Guiana and an expedition set sail up the Orinoco River to search for gold mines. Raleigh was too ill to accompany them and stayed with his ships to protect them from Spanish raiding parties. The river expedition was ambushed by the Spanish and, against express instructions, they retaliated. Wat Raleigh was mortally wounded, and many men were lost. No gold mines were discovered. The failed expedition returned to Raleigh who was heartbroken to hear of the loss of his son. He returned to England a broken man.

Escape

On arrival in Plymouth, Raleigh attempted to escape to France but changed his mind as this action was not that of a man of honour. He was arrested and escorted to London. At Salisbury, he feigned illness for he needed time to fine-tune his defence and write his 'Apology'. He was supplied with ointment, which made him look like a leper and he rubbed the inside of his chamber pot with a chemical, which made his urine turn black. To further corroborate his illness, he let it be known that he had not eaten for three days. In fact, he ate a leg of mutton and three loaves. Sadly, James did not read the 'Apology' during Raleigh's lifetime.

A plan was then hatched by the King of France to employ Raleigh to help in France's struggle with its arch-enemy, Spain. Raleigh set off from Tower Dock in a rowing boat, disguised in a false beard, a hat and cloak, and armed with four pistols, with the intention of meeting a ship bound for France at Gravesend. However, he was betrayed and captured, and he entered the Tower for final time on 10th August 1618. A trial was held in private, and Raleigh was once more found guilty of treason and sentenced to be hung, drawn and quartered. James commuted this death to beheading. His execution could be seen as redress to the Spanish.

A portrait of Raleigh painted in the Tower of London just before his execution. Raleigh is still sporting a sun tan from his trip to Guiana.

An aerial view of the Houses of Parliament in Westminster showing Old Palace Yard where Sir Walter Raleigh was executed.

Execution

The date for Raleigh's death – 29th October 1618 – was specifically chosen as it coincided with the Lord Mayor's Show. It was hoped that the mob would be distracted. Pleas for clemency were urgently made by Bess and his supporters, but to no avail. On a raw autumn morning, he was taken to the Old Palace Yard in Westminster. On the way to the scaffold, he gave his nightcap to an old man saying, 'Thou hast more need of it now than I'. He took some wine and smoked a pipe and addressed the crowd with much theatrics for half an hour, expressing his innocence. As he prepared himself for death, he ran his finger along the edge of the axe and said, 'This is sharp medicine, but it is a physician that will cure all my diseases.' And upon the hesitation of the executioner he shouted, 'Strike, man, strike!'

Pipe smoked by Raleigh on the scaffold.

He was buried in St. Margaret's, Westminster, and Bess, his wife, carried his embalmed head around with her in a red velvet bag for the next 29 years. This was later interred next to his body alongside that of his son, Carew, in 1667.

Execution of Sir Walter Raleigh.

His Legend

Four hundred years after his death, Raleigh remains one of the best-known figures of his time. A BBC survey in 2002 to find the Greatest Britons placed him at number 93, alongside such luminaries as Isambard Kingdom Brunel, Isaac Newton and Margaret Thatcher. He was perhaps one of the last true Renaissance men and one of the founding fathers of the British Empire. The longevity of his appeal is based on his many characteristics that speak to us across the ages: adventurer, explorer, and swashbuckling pirate. He is remembered as the loyal friend of a queen and for his infamous imprisonment and execution.

His writings, particularly *The Historie of the World* were essential books in any gentleman's library on both sides of the Atlantic. Throughout the ensuing centuries, they have been continually referenced. William Shakespeare, Oliver Cromwell and Milton all quoted his writings. His appeal stretches to both sides of The Pond: he is immortalised on the $10 coin, and the capital of North Carolina is named after him.

The brand RALEIGH has been used to promote various products including, tobacco, pubs, drinks and flowers. Raleigh International, named to commemorate Sir Walter Raleigh's first colonising expedition to America, in 1584, provides young explorers with a chance to see the world.

The Sir Walter Raleigh Pub in East Budleigh.

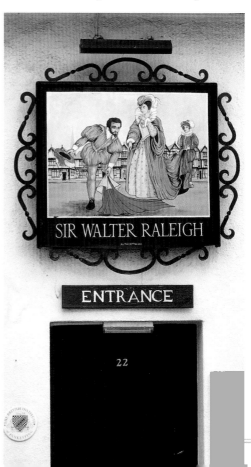

Film, Television and Song

The Elizabethan era has long been a subject for film makers. Raleigh has been portrayed by Richard Todd, in the 1955 production of *The Virgin Queen* and by Clive Owen in *Elizabeth: The Golden Age* in 2007. Simon Jones's portrayal of him in *Blackadder* celebrates what he is most widely known for: the potato. His legend was immortalised in the Beatles lyric that links him to tobacco.

'Although I'm so tired I'll have another cigarette/And curse Sir Walter Raleigh/ He was such a stupid git'

From *The White Album*

Conclusion

Walter Raleigh's life helped to define the Elizabethan age. In life and death, his story rides fortune's roller coaster. However, behind the façade of one of British history's favourite characters emerges a more complex figure. History remembers him as a great seafarer who introduced potatoes, tobacco and smoking to England, yet his greatest achievements were on land. He crossed dangerous oceans in search of new lands and fortune, and risked his life and money for the glory of his queen. He has been called the founding father of the British Empire, although paradoxically he never actually set foot in North America. He acted out his career on the international stage but kept his Devon accent all his life. He was ruthless in battle and in the pursuit of his career, yet he wrote profoundly moving poetry, which is still read today. Every aspect of his life is marked by ambition although, unsurprisingly, not everything he did resulted in success.

The Raleigh statue in East Budleigh.

'He was fortune's tennis ball'

His estates in Ireland were never profitable, his settlement in Virginia did not take permanent root and his expeditions left him out of pocket. Two attempts to find the fabled El Dorado were unsuccessful, and the second one ended in disaster. His great work, *The Historie of the World*, was never completed.

With the death of Queen Elizabeth, Raleigh's luck ran out. He was unable to embrace the politics of the new King, James I, who viewed him with suspicion. His involvement in a conspiracy against the King led to his arrest, trial and sentence to death for treason. At the height of his career, he was despised as a grasping upstart who was ambitious for Queen Elizabeth's favour, yet after his fall from grace when he was imprisoned in the Tower of London, he became a national hero and a symbol of a lost Golden Age. He died a political martyr, and in death achieved the glory he had been denied in life. His life story has all the ingredients of a true swashbuckling adventure: romance, daring, exploration and panache.

At his execution the axeman allegedly uttered, 'Behold the head of a traitor' and a voice from the crowd called,

'We have not another such head to be cut off.'

Places to Visit

Step back in time and follow in the footsteps of Sir Walter Raleigh

Burghley House, Stamford, Lincolnshire, PE9 3JY www.burghley.co.uk

Dents, Furnax Lane, Warminster, Wiltshire BA12 8PE www.dents.co.uk

Fairlynch Museum & Arts Centre, Budleigh Salterton, Devon EX9 6NP www.fairlynchmuseum.uk

Middle Temple, Middle Temple Lane, London, EC4Y 9BT www.middletemple.org.uk

Oriel College, Oxford OX1 4EW www.oriel.ox.ac.uk

Petworth House and Park, Petworth, West Sussex, GU28 9LR
https://www.nationaltrust.org.uk/petworth-house-and-park

Sherborne Castle, New Road, Sherborne, Dorset DT9 5NR www.sherbornecastle.com

Sherborne Old Castle, Castleton, Sherborne, Dorset DT9 3SA
www.english-heritage.org.uk/visit/places/sherborne-old-castle/

The Tower of London, London, EC3N 4AB www.hrp.org.uk/toweroflondon

The Maritime Museum Greenwich, Park Row, Greenwich, London, SE10 9NF
www.rmg.co.uk/national-maritime-museum

The Hall at
Sherborne
Castle.